AMICUS ILLUSTRATED • AMICUS

DO YOU REALLY WANT TO MEET
A CAMEL?

WRITTEN BY BRIDGET HEOS   ILLUSTRATED BY DANIELE FABBRI

Amicus Illustrated and Amicus Ink
are imprints of Amicus
P.O. Box 1329
Mankato, MN 56002

Library of Congress Cataloging-in-Publication Data
Names: Heos, Bridget, author. | Fabbri, Daniele, 1978-
illustrator.
Title: Do you really want to meet a camel? / by Bridget
Heos ; illustrated by Daniele Fabbri.
Description: Mankato, MN : Amicus Illustrated, [2016]
| Series: Do you really want to meet...wild animals? |
Audience: K to grade 3. | Description based on print
version record and CIP data provided by publisher;
resource not viewed.
Identifiers: LCCN 2015034253 (print) |
LCCN 2015037109 (ebook) |
ISBN 9781607539452 (library binding) |
ISBN 9781681521169 (pbk.) |
ISBN 9781681510637 (ebook)
Subjects: LCSH: Bactrian camel—Behavior—Juvenile
literature. | Camels—Juvenile literature.
Classification: LCC SF401.C2 (print) | LCC SF401.C2
H46 2016 (ebook) | DDC 599.63/62—dc23
LC record available at http://lccn.loc.gov/2015034253

Editor: Rebecca Glaser
Designer: Kathleen Petelinsek

Printed in the United States of America at Corporate
Graphics in North Mankato, Minnesota.

HC 10 9 8 7 6 5 4 3 2 1
PB 10 9 8 7 6 5 4 3 2 1

ABOUT THE AUTHOR

Bridget Heos lives in Kansas City with her husband, four
children, and an extremely dangerous cat . . . to mice,
anyway. She has written more than 80 books for children,
including many about animals. Find out more about her at
www.authorbridgetheos.com.

ABOUT THE ILLUSTRATOR

Daniele Fabbri was born in Ravenna, Italy, in 1978. He
graduated from Istituto Europeo di Design in Milan, Italy,
and started his career as a cartoon animator, storyboarder,
and background designer for animated series. He has
worked as a freelance illustrator since 2003, collaborating
with international publishers and advertising agencies.

amels are amazing animals. Wouldn't it be fun to meet one in the wild? You would have to go to the freezing Gobi Desert— the only place wild camels still live. Are you up for that?

Okay, let's go. The Gobi Desert is in Mongolia and China. From California, a plane ride to the capital of Mongolia, Ulan Bator, will take a day. And our journey will not end there!

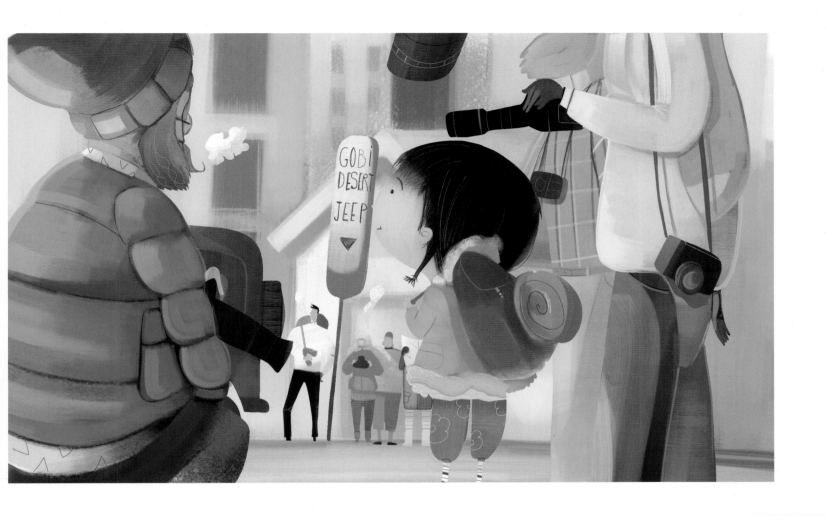

Wild camels are rare. So we're traveling with
photographers who are doing a story on wild
camels. There's our group!

It takes three and one-half days to drive to the
wildlife preserve. There aren't many paved
roads. So it's a bumpy ride!

Hey, there's a herd of camels. But they're not wild. These camels are domesticated. Here, families raise camels for their meat, milk, and fur. Let's go meet them!

The family lives in a *ger*. Its walls are covered with felt. At the center, a stove burns camel dung (dried poop). That means it's cozy inside. The people offer us milk and cheese, which comes from the camels, too. Yum! Camel milk is delicious.

Would you like to ride one of the camels? It's a fun and cozy ride, sitting between the camel's humps. But now it's getting dark.

We're in luck. The family has invited us to stay the night. We feast on camel meat and sleep under warm camel hair blankets!

Now it's morning. Time to continue our journey! The Gobi Desert is cold and dry. It's hard to find food and water. Do you know how camels survive?

They don't store water in their humps. But they do store fat. When a camel can't find food or water, it lives off the fat. Camels can go for days without food.

There are two types of camels. A one-hump, or dromedary, camel lives in Africa, the Middle East, and Australia. They have all been domesticated.

The camels that live in the Gobi Desert are Bactrian camels. They have two humps. There are only about 1,000 left in the wild. Let's hope we see one!

Finally, here's the wildlife preserve. Camels have their fur to keep warm. But we need a fire! There isn't much firewood around. The Mongolian family burned dung for heat. Maybe we could, too! And if there's camel dung, the camels must be nearby!

Look! Wild camels! Camels graze all day in family groups of up to 30. They're herbivores, so they only eat plants.

These camels have never seen people.
They're curious about us, too.

Hello there, wild camels!

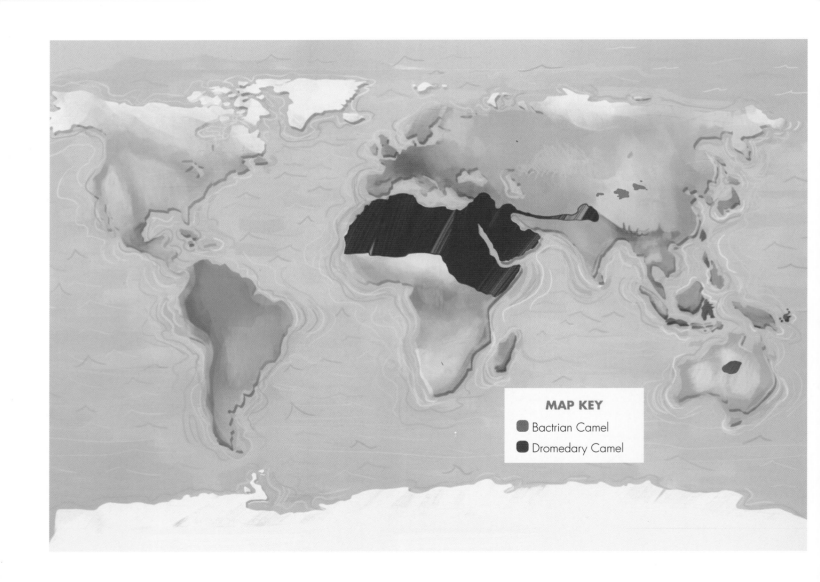

MAP KEY
- Bactrian Camel
- Dromedary Camel

GLOSSARY

Bactrian camel A two-hump camel that lives in Asia.

domesticated Raised by humans over several generations, so that an animal is no longer wild.

dromedary camel A one-hump camel, also known as the Arabian camel; all dromedary camels have been domesticated.

dung Animal poop.

ger A circular tent made of felt or skins, also called a yurt.

herbivore An animal that eats plants as its main diet.

READ MORE

Allgor, Marie. *Endangered Desert Animals*. New York: PowerKids Press, 2013.

Gish, Melissa. Camels. Mankato, Minn.: Creative Paperbacks, 2013.

Goldish, Meish. **Camel**. New York: Bearport Publishing, 2015.

Turnbull, Stephanie. Camel. Mankato, Minn.: Smart Apple Media, 2015.

WEBSITES

ARKive: Wild Bactrian Camels
http://www.arkive.org/wild-bactrian-camel/camelus-ferus/
See photos and watch video clips of Bactrian camels in the wild.

Easy Science for Kids: Deserts of the World
http://easyscienceforkids.com/all-about-deserts/
Learn more about deserts like the Gobi.

National Geographic Kids: Bactrian Camel
http://kids.nationalgeographic.com/animals/bactrian-camel/
Learn more about two-hump camels.

San Diego Zoo: Camel
http://animals.sandiegozoo.org/animals/camel
Learn more about all kinds of camels.

Every effort has been made to ensure that these websites are appropriate for children. However, because of the nature of the Internet, it is impossible to guarantee that these sites will remain active indefinitely or that their contents will not be altered.